THE GREATEST THING

IN

THE WORLD

AN ADDRESS

by

HENRY DRUMMOND

Afterword by

DENIS DUNCAN

HODDER AND STOUGHTON
LONDON SYDNEY AUCKLAND TORONTO

British Library Cataloguing in Publication Data

Drummond, Henry
  The greatest thing in the world.
  1. Bible.   New Testament.   Corinthians 1 XIII –
  Commentaries
  I. Title
  227'.2   BS2675.3

ISBN 0–340–22819–9

Note to First Edition

TRANSLATIONS of this Address having found their way into several foreign languages, this English edition, corrected from the original stenographer's report, is now published by request.

Though I speak with the tongues of men and of angels, and have not Love, I am become as sounding brass, or a tinkling cymbal. And though I have the gift of prophecy, and understand all mysteries, and all knowledge; and though I have all faith, so that I could remove mountains, and have not Love, I am nothing. And though I bestow all my goods to feed the poor, and though I give my body to be burned, and have not Love, it profiteth me nothing.

Love suffereth long, and is kind;
Love envieth not;
Love vaunteth not itself, is not puffed up,
Doth not behave itself unseemly,
Seeketh not her own,
Is not easily provoked,
Thinketh no evil;
Rejoiceth not in inquity, but rejoiceth in the truth;
Beareth all things, believeth all things,
hopeth all things, endureth all things.

Love never faileth: but whether there be prophecies, they shall fail; whether there be tongues, they shall cease; whether there be knowledge, it shall vanish away. For we know in part, and we prophesy in part. But when that which is perfect is come, then that which is in part shall be done away. When I was a child, I spake as a child, I understood as a child, I thought as a child: but when I became a man, I put away childish things. For now we see through a glass, darkly; but then face to face: now I know in part; but then shall I know even as also I am known. And now abideth faith, hope, Love, these three; but the greatest of these is Love.—I COR. xiii.

THE GREATEST THING IN THE WORLD

EVERYONE has asked himself the great question of antiquity as of the modern world: What is the *summum bonum*—the supreme good? You have life before you. Once only you can live it. What is the noblest object of desire, the supreme gift to covet?

We have been accustomed to be told that the greatest thing in the religious world is Faith. That great word has been the key-note for centuries of the popular religion; and we have easily learned to look upon it as the greatest thing in the world. Well, we are wrong. If we have been told that, we may miss the mark. I have taken you, in the chapter which I have just read, to Christianity at its source; and there we have seen, "The greatest of these is Love." It is not an oversight. Paul was speaking of faith just a moment before. He says, "If I have all faith, so that I can remove mountains, and have not love, I am nothing." So far from forgetting he deliberately contrasts them, "Now abideth Faith, Hope, Love," and without a moment's hesitation the decision falls, "The greatest of these is Love."

And it is not prejudice. A man is apt to recommend to others his own strong point. Love was not Paul's strong point. The observing student can detect a beautiful tenderness growing and ripening all through his character as Paul gets old; but the hand that wrote, "The greatest of these is Love," when we meet it first, is stained with blood.

Nor is this letter to the Corinthians peculiar in singling out Love as the *summum bonum*. The masterpieces of Christianity are agreed about it. Peter says, "Above all things have fervent Love among yourselves." *Above all things.* And John goes farther, "God is Love." And you remember the profound remark which Paul makes elsewhere, "Love is the fulfilling of the law." Did you ever think what he meant by that? In those days men were working their passage to Heaven by keeping the Ten Commandments, and the hundred and ten other commandments which they had manufactured out of them. Christ said, I will show you a more simple way. If you do one thing, you will do these hundred and ten things, without ever thinking about them. If you love, you will unconsciously fulfil the whole law. And you can readily see for yourselves how that must be so. Take any of the commandments. "Thou shalt have no other gods before Me." If a man love God, you will not require to tell him that? Love is the fulfilling of that law. "Take not His name in vain." Would he ever dream of taking His name in vain if he loved Him? "Remember the Sabbath day to keep it holy." Would he not be too glad to have one day in seven to dedicate more exclusively to the object of his affection? Love would fulfil all these laws regarding God. And so, if he loved Man, you would never think of telling him to honour his father and mother. He could not do anything else. It would be preposterous to tell him not to kill. You could only insult him if you suggested that he should not steal—how could he steal from those he loved? It would be superfluous to beg him not to bear false witness against his neighbour. If he loved him it would be the last thing he would do. And you would never dream of urging him not to covet what his neighbours had. He would rather they possessed it than himself. In this way "Love is the fulfilling of the law." It is the rule for fulfilling all rules, the new commandment for keeping all the old commandments, Christ's one secret of the Christian life.

Now Paul had learned that; and in this noble eulogy he has given us the most wonderful and original account extant of the *summum bonum*. We may divide it into three parts. In the beginning of the short chapter, we have Love *contrasted*; in the heart of it, we have Love *analysed*; towards the end, we have Love *defended* as the supreme gift.

THE CONTRAST

PAUL begins by contrasting Love with other things that men in those days thought much of. I shall not attempt to go over those things in detail. Their inferiority is already obvious.

He contrasts it with eloquence. And what a noble gift it is, the power of playing upon the souls and wills of men, and rousing them to lofty purposes and holy deeds. Paul says, "If I speak with the tongues of men and of angels, and have not Love, I am become as sounding brass, or a tinkling cymbal." And we all know why. We have all felt the brazenness of words without emotion, the hollowness, the unaccountable unpersuasiveness, of eloquence behind which lies no Love.

He contrasts it with prophecy. He contrasts it with mysteries. He contrasts it with faith. He contrasts it with charity. Why is Love greater than faith? Because the end is greater than the means. And why is it greater than charity? Because the whole is greater than the part. Love is greater than faith, because the end is greater than the means. What is the use of having faith? It is to connect the soul with God. And what is the object of connecting man with God? That he may become like God. But God is Love. Hence faith, the means, is in order to Love, the end. Love, therefore, obviously is greater than faith. It is greater than charity, again, because the whole is greater than a part. Charity is only a little bit of Love, one of the innumerable avenues of Love, and there may even be, and there is, a great deal of charity without Love. It is a very easy thing to toss a copper to a beggar on the street; it is generally an easier thing than not to do it. Yet Love is just as often in the withholding. We purchase relief from the sympathetic feelings roused by the spectacle of misery, at the copper's cost. It is too cheap—too cheap for us, and often too dear for the beggar. If we really loved him we would either do more for him, or less.

Then Paul contrasts it with sacrifice and martyrdom. And I beg the little band of would-be missionaries—and I have the honour to call some of you by this name for the first time—to remember that though you give your bodies to be burned, and have not Love, it profits nothing—nothing! You can take nothing greater to the heathen world than the impress and reflection of the Love of God upon your own character. That is the universal language. It will take you years to speak in Chinese, or in the dialects of India. From the day you land, that language of Love, understood by all, will be pouring forth its unconscious eloquence. It is the man who is the missionary, it is not his words. His character is his message. In the heart of Africa, among the great Lakes, I have come across black men and women who remembered the only white man they ever saw before—David Livingstone; and as you cross his footsteps in that dark continent, men's faces light up as they speak of the kind Doctor who passed there years ago. They could not understand him; but they felt the Love that beat in his heart. Take into your new sphere of labour, where you also mean to lay down your life, that simple charm, and your lifework must succeed. You can take nothing greater, you need take nothing less. It is not worth while going if you take anything less. You may take every accomplishment; you may be braced for every sacrifice; but if you give your body to be burned, and have not Love, it will profit you and the cause of Christ *nothing*.

THE ANALYSIS

AFTER contrasting Love with these things, Paul, in three verses, very short, gives us an amazing analysis of what this supreme thing is. I ask you to look at it. It is a compound thing, he tells us. It is like light. As you have seen a man of science take a beam of light and pass it through a crystal prism, as you have seen it come out on the other side of the prism broken up into its component colours— red, and blue, and yellow, and violet, and orange, and all the colours of the rainbow—so Paul passes this thing, Love, through the magnificent prism of his inspired intellect, and it comes out on the other side broken up into its elements. And in these few words we have what one might call the Spectrum of Love, the analysis of Love. Will you observe what its elements are? Will you notice that they have common names; that they are virtues which we hear about every day, that they are things which can be practised by every man in every place in life; and how, by a multitude of small things and ordinary virtues, the supreme thing, the *summum bonum*, is made up?

The Spectrum of Love has nine ingredients:

Patience	"Love suffereth long."
Kindness	"And is kind."
Generosity	"Love envieth not."
Humility	"Love vaunteth not itself, is not puffed up."
Courtesy	"Doth not behave itself unseemly."
Unselfishness	"Seeketh not her own."
Good Temper.	"Is not easily provoked."
Guilelessness	"Thinketh no evil."
Sincerity	"Rejoiceth not in iniquity, but rejoiceth in the truth."

Patience; kindness; generosity; humility; courtesy; unselfishness; good temper; guilelessness; sincerity—these make up the supreme gift, the stature of the perfect man. You will observe that all are in relation to men, in relation to life, in relation to the known to-day and the near to-morrow, and not to the unknown eternity. We hear much of Love to God; Christ spoke much of Love to man. We make a great deal of peace with heaven; Christ made much of peace on earth. Religion is not a strange or added thing, but the inspiration of the secular life, the breathing of an eternal spirit through this temporal world. The supreme thing, in short, is not a thing at all, but the giving of a further finish to the multitudinous words and acts which make up the sum of every common day.

There is no time to do more than make a passing note upon each of these ingredients. Love is *Patience*. This is the normal attitude of Love; Love passive, Love waiting to begin; not in a hurry; calm; ready to do its work when the summons comes, but meantime wearing the ornament of a meek and quiet spirit. Love suffers long; beareth all things; believeth all things; hopeth all things. For Love understands, and therefore awaits.

Kindness. Love active. Have you ever noticed how much of Christ's life was spent in doing kind things—in *merely* doing kind things? Run over it with that in view, and you will find that He spent a great proportion of His time simply in making people happy, in doing good turns to people. There is only one thing greater than happiness in the world, and that is holiness; and it is not in our keeping; but what God *has* put in our power is the happiness of those about us, and that is largely to be secured by our being kind to them.

"The greatest thing," says someone, "a man can

do for his Heavenly Father is to be kind to some of His other children." I wonder why it is that we are not all kinder than we are? How much the world needs it. How easily it is done. How instantaneously it acts. How infallibly it is remembered. How superabundantly it pays itself back—for there is no debtor in the world so honourable, so superbly honourable, as Love. "Love never faileth." Love is success, Love is happiness, Love is life. "Love, I say," with Browning, "is energy of Life."

"For life, with all it yields of joy and woe
  And hope and fear,
  Is just our chance o' the prize of learning love—
  How love might be, hath been indeed, and is."

Where Love is, God is. He that dwelleth in Love dwelleth in God. God is Love. Therefore *love*. Without distinction, without calculation, without procrastination, love. Lavish it upon the poor, where it is very easy; especially upon the rich, who often need it most; most of all upon our equals, where it is very difficult, and for whom perhaps we each do least of all. There is a difference between *trying to please* and *giving pleasure*. Give pleasure. Lose no chance of giving pleasure. For that is the ceaseless and anonymous triumph of a truly loving spirit. "I shall pass through this world but once. Any good thing therefore that I can do, or any kindness that I can show to any human being, let me do it now. Let me not defer it or neglect it, for I shall not pass this way again."

Generosity. "Love envieth not." This is Love in competition with others. Whenever you attempt a good work you will find other men doing the same kind of work, and probably doing it better. Envy them not. Envy is a feeling of ill-will to those who are in the same line as ourselves, a spirit of covetousness and detraction. How little Christian work even is a protection against un-Christian feeling. That most despicable of all the unworthy moods which cloud a Christian's soul assuredly waits for us on the threshold of every work, unless we are fortified with this grace of magnanimity. Only one thing truly need the Christian envy, the large, rich, generous soul which "envieth not".

And then, after having learned all that, you have to learn this further thing, *Humility*—to put a seal upon your lips and forget what you have done. After you have been kind, after Love has stolen forth into the world and done its beautiful work, go back into the shade again and say nothing about it. Love hides even from itself. Love waives even self-satisfaction. "Love vaunteth not itself, is not puffed up."

The fifth ingredient is a somewhat strange one to find in this *summum bonum*: *Courtesy*. This is Love in society, Love in relation to etiquette. "Love doth not behave itself unseemly." Politeness has been defined as Love in trifles. Courtesy is said to be Love in little things. And the one secret of politeness is to Love. Love *cannot* behave itself unseemly. You can put the most untutored person into the highest society, and if they have a reservoir of Love in their heart, they will not behave themselves unseemly. They simply cannot do it. Carlyle said of Robert Burns that there was no truer gentleman in Europe than the ploughman-poet. It was because he loved everything—the mouse, and the daisy, and all the things, great and small, that God had made. So with this simple passport he could mingle with any society, and enter courts and palaces from his little cottage on the banks of the Ayr. You know the meaning of the word "gentleman". It means a gentle man—a man who does things gently, with Love. And that is the whole art and mystery of it.

The gentle man cannot in the nature of things do an ungentle, an ungentlemanly thing. The ungentle soul, the inconsiderate, unsympathetic nature cannot do anything else. "Love doth not behave itself unseemly."

Unselfishness. "Love seeketh not her own." Observe: Seeketh not even that which is her own. In Britain the Englishman is devoted, and rightly, to his rights. But there come times when a man may exercise even the higher right of giving up his rights. Yet Paul does not summon us to give up our rights. Love strikes much deeper. It would have us not seek them at all, ignore them, eliminate the personal element altogether from our calculations. It is not hard to give up our rights. They are often external. The difficult thing is to give up ourselves. The more difficult thing still is not to seek things for ourselves at all. After we have sought them, bought them, won them, deserved them, we have taken the cream off them for ourselves already. Little cross then perhaps to give them up. But not to seek them, to look every man not on his own things, but on the things of others—*id opus est.* "Seekest thou great things for thyself?" said the prophet; "*seek them not.*" Why? Because there is no greatness in *things*. Things cannot be great. The only greatness is unselfish Love. Even self-denial in itself is nothing, is almost a mistake. Only a great purpose or a mightier Love can justify the waste. It is more difficult, I have said, not to seek our own at all, than, having sought it, to give it up. I must take that back. It is only true of a partly selfish heart. Nothing is a hardship to Love, and nothing is hard. I believe that Christ's yoke is easy. Christ's "yoke" is just His way of taking life. And I believe it is an easier way than any other. I believe it is a happier way than any other. The most obvious lesson in Christ's teaching is that there is no happiness in having and getting anything, but only in giving. I repeat, *there is no happiness in having or in getting, but only in giving.* And half the world is on the wrong scent in the pursuit of happiness. They think it consists in having and getting, and in being served by others. It consists in giving, and in serving others. He that would be great among you, said Christ, let him serve. He that would be happy, let him remember that there is but one way—it is more blessed, it is more happy, to give than to receive.

The next ingredient is a very remarkable one: *Good Temper.* "Love is not easily provoked."

Nothing could be more striking than to find this here. We are inclined to look upon bad temper as a very harmless weakness. We speak of it as a mere infirmity of nature, a family failing, a matter of temperament, not a thing to take into very serious account in estimating a man's character. And yet here, right in the heart of this analysis of Love, it finds a place; and the Bible again and again returns to condemn it as one of the most destructive elements in human nature.

The peculiarity of ill temper is that it is the vice of the virtuous. It is often the one blot on an otherwise noble character. You know men who are all but perfect, and women who would be entirely perfect, but for an easily ruffled, quick-tempered, or "touchy" disposition. This compatibility of ill temper with high moral character is one of the strangest and saddest problems of ethics. The truth is there are two great classes of sins—sins of the *Body*, and sins of the *Disposition*. The Prodigal Son may be taken as a type of the first, the Elder Brother of the second. Now society has no doubt whatever as to which of these is the worse. Its brand falls, without a challenge, upon the Prodigal. But are we right? We have no balance to weigh one another's sins, and coarser and finer are but human words; but faults in the higher nature may be less venial than those in the lower, and to the eye of Him who is Love, a sin against Love may seem a hundred times more base. No form of vice, not worldliness, not greed of gold, not drunkenness itself, does more to un-Christianise society than evil temper. For embittering life, for breaking up communities, for destroying the most sacred relationships, for devastating homes, for withering up men and women, for taking the bloom off childhood, in short, for sheer gratuitous misery-producing power, this influence stands alone. Look at the Elder Brother, moral, hard-working, patient, dutiful—let him get all credit for his virtues—look at this man, this baby, sulking outside his own father's door. "He was angry," we read, "and would not go in." Look at the effect upon the father, upon the servants, upon the happiness of the guests. Judge of the effect upon the Prodigal—and how many prodigals are kept out of the Kingdom of God by the unlovely characters of those who profess to be inside? Analyse, as a study in temper, the thunder-cloud itself as it gathers upon the Elder Brother's brow. What is it made of? Jealousy, anger, pride, uncharity, cruelty, self-righteousness, touchiness, doggedness, sullenness—these are the ingredients of this dark and loveless soul. In varying proportions, also, these are the ingredients of all ill temper. Judge if such sins of the disposition are not worse to live in, and for others to live with, than sins of the body. Did Christ indeed not answer the question Himself when He said, "I say unto you, that the publicans and the harlots go into the Kingdom of Heaven before you." There is really no place in Heaven for a disposition like this. A man with such a mood could only make Heaven miserable for all the people in it. Except, therefore, such a man be born again, he cannot, he simply *cannot*, enter the Kingdom of Heaven. For it is perfectly certain—and you will not misunderstand me—that to enter Heaven a man must take it with him.

You will see then why temper is significant. It is not in what it is alone, but in what it reveals. This is why I take the liberty now of speaking of it with such unusual plainness. It is a test for Love, a symptom, a revelation of an unloving nature at bottom. It is the intermittent fever which bespeaks unintermittent disease within; the occasional bubble

escaping to the surface which betrays some rotten-
ness underneath; a sample of the most hidden
products of the soul dropped involuntarily when
off one's guard; in a word, the lightning form of a
hundred hideous and un-Christian sins. For a
want of patience, a want of kindness, a want of
generosity, a want of courtesy, a want of unselfishness, are all instantaneously symbolised in one flash
of temper.

Hence it is not enough to deal with the temper.
We must go to the source, and change the inmost
nature, and the angry humours will die away of
themselves. Souls are made sweet, not by taking the
acid fluids out, but by putting something in—a
great Love, a new Spirit, the Spirit of Christ.
Christ, the Spirit of Christ, interpenetrating ours,
sweetens, purifies, transforms all. This only can
eradicate what is wrong, work a chemical change,
renovate and regenerate, and rehabilitate the inner
man. Will-power does not change men. Time does
not change men. Christ does. Therefore "Let that
mind be in you which was also in Christ Jesus."
Some of us have not much time to lose. Remember,
once more, that this is a matter of life or death. I
cannot help speaking urgently, for myself, for

yourselves. "Whoso shall offend one of these little ones, which believe in me, it were better for him that a millstone were hanged about his neck, and that he were drowned in the depth of the sea." That is to say, it is the deliberate verdict of the Lord Jesus that it is better not to live than not to love. *It is better not to live than not to love.*

Guilelessness and *Sincerity* may be dismissed almost with a word. Guilelessness is the grace for suspicious people. And the possession of it is the great secret of personal influence. You will find, if you think for a moment, that the people who influence you are people who believe in you. In an atmosphere of suspicion men shrivel up; but in that atmosphere they expand, and find encouragement and educative fellowship. It is a wonderful thing that here and there in this hard, uncharitable world there should still be left a few rare souls who think no evil. This is the great unworldliness. Love "thinketh no evil", imputes no motive, sees the bright side, puts the best construction on every action. What a delightful state of mind to live in! What a stimulus and benediction even to meet with it for a day! To be trusted is to be saved. And if we try to influence or elevate others, we shall soon see that success is in proportion to their belief of our belief in them. For the respect of another is the first restoration of the self-respect a man has lost; our ideal of what he is becomes to him the hope and pattern of what he may become.

"Love rejoiceth not in iniquity, but rejoiceth in the truth." I have called this *Sincerity* from the words rendered in the Authorised Version by "rejoiceth in the truth". And, certainly, were this the real translation, nothing could be more just. For he who loves will love truth not less than men. He will rejoice in the truth—rejoice not in what he has been taught to believe; not in this Church's doctrine or in that; not in this ism or in that ism; but "in *the truth*". He will accept only what is real; he will strive to get at facts; he will search for *truth* with a humble and unbiassed mind, and cherish whatever he finds at any sacrifice. But the more literal translation of the Revised Version calls for just such a sacrifice for truth's sake here. For what Paul really meant is, as we there read, "Rejoiceth not in unrighteousness, but rejoiceth with the truth," a quality which probably no one English word—and certainly not *Sincerity*—adequately defines. It includes, perhaps more strictly, the self-restraint which refuses to make capital out of others' faults; the charity which delights not in exposing the weakness of others, but "covereth all things"; the sincerity of purpose which endeavours to see things as they are, and rejoices to find them better than suspicion feared or calumny denounced.

So much for the analysis of Love. Now the business of our lives is to have these things fitted into our characters. That is the supreme work to which we need to address ourselves in this world, to learn Love. Is life not full of opportunities for learning Love? Every man and woman every day has a thousand of them. The world is not a playground; it is a schoolroom. Life is not a holiday, but an education. And the one eternal lesson for us all is *how better we can love*. What makes a man a good cricketer? Practice. What makes a man a good artist, a good sculptor, a good musician? Practice. What makes a man a good linguist, a good stenographer? Practice. What makes a man a good man? Practice. Nothing else. There is nothing capricious about religion. We do not get the soul in different ways, under different laws, from those in which we get the body and the mind. If a man does not exercise his arm he develops no biceps muscle; and if a man does not exercise his soul, he acquires no muscle in his soul, no strength of character, no vigour of moral fibre, nor beauty of spiritual growth. Love is not a thing of enthusiastic emotion. It is a rich, strong, manly, vigorous expression of the whole round Christian character —the Christlike nature in its fullest development. And the constituents of this great character are only to be built up by ceaseless practice.

What was Christ doing in the carpenter's shop? Practising. Though perfect, we read that He *learned* obedience, He *increased* in wisdom and in favour with God and man. Do not quarrel therefore with your lot in life. Do not complain of its never-ceasing cares, its petty environment, the vexations you have to stand, the small and sordid souls you have to live and work with. Above all, do not resent temptation; do not be perplexed because it seems to thicken round you more and more, and ceases neither for effort nor for agony nor prayer. That is the practice which God appoints you; and it is having its work in making you patient, and humble, and generous, and unselfish, and kind, and courteous. Do not grudge the hand that is moulding the still too shapeless image within you.

It is growing more beautiful, though you see it not, and every touch of temptation may add to its perfection. Therefore keep in the midst of life. Do not isolate yourself. Be among men, and among things, and among troubles, and difficulties, and obstacles. You remember Goethe's words: *Es bildet ein Talent sich in der Stille, Doch ein Character in dem Strom der Welt.* "Talent develops itself in solitude; character in the stream of life." Talent develops itself in solitude—the talent of prayer, of faith, of meditation, of seeing the unseen; character grows in the stream of the world's life. That chiefly is where men are to learn Love.

How? Now, how? To make it easier, I have named a few of the elements of Love. But these are only elements. Love itself can never be defined. Light is a something more than the sum of its ingredients—a glowing, dazzling, tremulous ether. And Love is something more than all its elements —a palpitating, quivering, sensitive, living thing. By synthesis of all the colours, men can make whiteness, they cannot make light. By synthesis of all the virtues, men can make virtue, they cannot make Love. How then are we to have this transcendent living whole conveyed into our souls? We brace our wills to secure it. We try to copy those who have it. We lay down rules about it. We watch. We pray. But these things alone will not bring Love into our nature. Love is an *effect*. And only as we fulfil the right condition can we have the effect produced. Shall I tell you what the *cause* is?

If you turn to the Revised Version of the First Epistle of John you will find these words: "We love because He first loved us." "We love," not "We love *Him*." That is the way the old version has it, and it is quite wrong. "*We love*—because He first loved us." Look at that word "because". It is the *cause* of which I have spoken. "*Because* He first loved us," the effect follows that we love, we love Him, we love all men. We cannot help it. Because He loved us, we love, we love everybody. Our heart is slowly changed. Contemplate the Love of Christ, and you will love. Stand before that mirror, reflect Christ's character, and you will be changed into the same image from tenderness to tenderness. There is no other way. You cannot love to order. You can only look at the lovely object, and fall in love with it, and grow into likeness to it. And so look at this Perfect Character, this Perfect Life. Look at the great Sacrifice as He laid

down Himself, all through life, and upon the
Cross of Calvary; and you must love Him. And
loving Him, you must become like Him, Love
begets Love. It is a process of induction. Put a
piece of iron in the presence of an electrified body,
and that piece of iron for a time becomes electrified. It is changed into a temporary magnet in
the mere presence of a permanent magnet, and as
long as you leave the two side by side, they are both
magnets alike. Remain side by side with Him
who loved us, and gave Himself for us, and you
too will become a permanent magnet, a per-
manently attractive force; and like Him you will
draw all men unto you, like Him you will be
drawn unto all men. That is the inevitable effect
of Love. Any man who fulfils that cause must have
that effect produced in him. Try to give up the
idea that religion comes to us by chance, or by
mystery, or by caprice. It comes to us by natural
law, or by supernatural law, for all law is Divine.
Edward Irving went to see a dying boy once, and
when he entered the room he just put his hand on
the sufferer's head, and said, "My boy, God loves
you," and went away. And the boy started from his
bed, and called out to the people in the house,

'God loves me! God loves me!" It changed that boy. The sense that God loved him overpowered him, melted him down, and began the creating of a new heart in him. And that is how the Love of God melts down the unlovely heart in man, and begets in him the new creature, who is patient and humble and gentle and unselfish. And there is no other way to get it. There is no mystery about it. We love others, we love everybody, we love our enemies, because He first loved us.

THE DEFENCE

NOW I have a closing sentence or two to add about Paul's reason for singling out Love as the supreme possession. It is a very remarkable reason. In a single word it is this: *it lasts*. "Love," urges Paul, "never faileth." Then he begins again one of his marvellous lists of the great things of the day, and exposes them one by one. He runs over the things that men thought were going to last, and shows that they are all fleeting, temporary, passing away.

"Whether there be prophecies, they shall fail." It was the mother's ambition for her boy in those days that he should become a prophet. For hundreds of years God had never spoken by means of any prophet, and at that time the prophet was greater than the King. Men waited wistfully for another messenger to come, and hung upon his lips when he appeared as upon the very voice of God. Paul says, "Whether there be prophecies, they shall fail." This Book is full of prophecies. One by one they have "failed"; that is, having been fulfilled their work is finished; they have nothing more to do now in the world except to feed a devout man's faith.

Then Paul talks about tongues. That was another thing that was greatly coveted. "Whether there be tongues, they shall cease." As we all know, many, many centuries have passed since tongues have been known in this world. They have ceased. Take it in any sense you like. Take it, for illustration merely, as languages in general—a sense which was not in Paul's mind at all, and which though it cannot give us the specific lesson will point out the general truth. Consider the words in which these chapters were written—Greek. It has gone. Take the Latin —the other great tongue of those days. It ceased long ago. Look at the Indian language. It is ceasing. The language of Wales, of Ireland, of the Scottish Highlands is dying before our eyes. The most popular book in the English tongue at the present time, except the Bible, is one of Dickens's works, his *Pickwick Papers*. It is largely written in the language of London street life; and experts assure us that in fifty years it will be unintelligible to the average English reader.

Then Paul goes farther, and with even greater boldness adds, "Whether there be knowledge, it shall vanish away." The wisdom of the ancients, where is it? It is wholly gone. A schoolboy to-day

37

knows more than Sir Isaac Newton knew. His knowledge has vanished away. You put yesterday's newspaper in the fire. Its knowledge has vanished away. You buy the old editions of the great encyclopaedias for a few pence. Their knowledge has vanished away. Look how the coach has been superseded by the use of steam. Look how electricity has superseded that, and swept a hundred almost new inventions into oblivion. One of the greatest living authorities, Sir William Thomson, said the other day, "The steam-engine is passing away." "Whether there be knowledge, it shall vanish away." At every workshop you will see, in the back yard, a heap of old iron, a few wheels, a few levers, a few cranks, broken and eaten with rust. Twenty years ago that was the pride of the city. Men flocked in from the country to see the great invention; now it is superseded, its day is done. And all the boasted science and philosophy of this day will soon be old. But yesterday, in the University of Edinburgh, the greatest figure in the faculty was Sir James Simpson, the discoverer of chloroform. The other day his successor and nephew, Professor Simpson, was asked by the librarian of the University to go to the library and pick out the books on his subject that were no longer needed. And his reply to the librarian was this: "Take every text-book that is more than ten years old, and put it down in the cellar." Sir James Simpson was a great authority only a few years ago: men came from all parts of the earth to consult him; and almost the whole teaching of that time is consigned by the science of to-day to oblivion. And in every branch of science it is the same. "Now we know in part. We see through a glass darkly."

Can you tell me anything that is going to last? Many things Paul did not condescend to name. He did not mention money, fortune, fame; but he picked out the great things of his time, the things the best men thought had something in them, and brushed them peremptorily aside. Paul had no charge against these things in themselves. All he said about them was that they would not last. They were great things, but not supreme things. There were things beyond them. What we are stretches past what we do, beyond what we possess. Many things that men denounce as sins are not sins; but they are temporary. And that is a favourite argument of the New Testament. John says of the world, not that it is wrong, but simply that it "passeth away". There is a great deal in the world that is delightful and beautiful; there is a great deal in it that is great and engrossing; but it will not last. All that is in the world, the lust of the eye, the lust of the flesh, and the pride of life, are but for a little while. Love not the world therefore. Nothing that it contains is worth the life and consecration of an immortal soul. The immortal soul must give itself to something that is immortal. And the only immortal things are these: "Now abideth faith, hope, Love, but the greatest of these is Love."

Some think the time may come when two of these three things will also pass away—faith into sight, hope into fruition. Paul does not say so. We know but little now about the conditions of the life that is to come. But what is certain is that Love must last. God, the Eternal God, is Love. Covet therefore that everlasting gift, that one thing which it is certain is going to stand, that one coinage which will be current in the Universe when all the other coinages of all the nations of the world shall be useless and unhonoured. You will give yourselves to many things, give yourselves first to Love. Hold things in their proportion. *Hold things in their proportion.* Let at least the first great object of our lives be to achieve the character defended in these words, the character—and it is the character of Christ—which is built round Love.

I have said this thing is eternal. Did you ever notice how continually John associates Love and faith with eternal life? I was not told when I was a boy that "God so loved the world that He gave His only begotten Son, that whosoever believeth in Him should have everlasting life." What I was told, I remember, was, that God so loved the world that, if I trusted in Him, I was to have a thing called peace, or I was to have rest, or I was to have joy, or I was to have safety. But I had to find out for myself that whosoever trusteth in Him—that is, whosoever loveth Him, for trust is only the avenue to Love—hath everlasting *life*. The Gospel offers a man life. Never offer men a thimbleful of Gospel. Do not offer them merely joy, or merely peace, or merely rest, or merely safety; tell them how Christ came to give men a more abundant life than they have, a life abundant in Love, and therefore abundant in salvation for themselves, and large in enterprise for the alleviation and redemption of the world. Then only can the Gospel take hold of the whole of a man, body, soul, and spirit, and give to each part of his nature its exercise and reward. Many of the current Gospels are addressed only to a part of man's nature. They offer peace, not life; faith, not Love; justification, not regeneration. And men slip back again from such religion because it has never really held them. Their nature was not all in it. It offered no deeper and gladder life-current than the life that was lived before. Surely it stands to reason that only a fuller Love can compete with the love of the world.

To love abundantly is to live abundantly, and to love for ever is to live for ever. Hence, eternal life is inextricably bound up with Love. We want to live for ever for the same reason that we want to live to-morrow. Why do you want to live to-morrow? It is because there is someone who loves you, and whom you want to see to-morrow, and be with, and love back. There is no other reason why we should live on than that we love and are beloved. It is when a man has no one to love him that he commits suicide. So long as he has friends, those who love him and whom he loves, he will live; because to live is to love. Be it but the love of a dog, it will keep him in life; but let that go and he has no contact with life, no reason to live. The "energy of life" has failed. Eternal life also is to know God, and God is Love. This is Christ's own definition. Ponder it. "This is life eternal, that they might know Thee the only true God, and Jesus Christ whom Thou hast sent." Love must be eternal. It is what God is. On the last analysis, then, Love is life. Love never faileth, and life never faileth, so long as there is Love. That is the philosophy of what Paul is showing us; the reason why in the nature of things Love should be the supreme thing—because it is going to last; because in the nature of things it is an Eternal Life. It is a thing that we are living now, not that we get when we die; that we shall have a poor chance of getting when we die unless we are living now. No worse fate can befall a man in this world than to live and grow old alone, unloving, and unloved. To be lost is to live in an unregenerate condition, loveless and unloved; and to be saved is to love; and he that dwelleth in Love dwelleth already in God. For God is Love.

Now I have all but finished. How many of you will join me in reading this chapter once a week for the next three months? A man did that once and it changed his whole life. Will you do it? It is for the greatest thing in the world. You might begin

43

by reading it every day, especially the verses which describe the perfect character. "Love suffereth long, and is kind; Love envieth not; Love vaunteth not itself." Get these ingredients into your life. Then everything that you do is eternal. It is worth doing. It is worth giving time to. No man can become a saint in his sleep; and to fulfil the condition required demands a certain amount of prayer and meditation and time, just as improvement in any direction, bodily or mental, requires preparation and care. Address yourselves to that one thing; at any cost have this transcendent character exchanged for yours. You will find as you look back upon your life that the moments that stand out, the moments when you have really lived, are the moments when you have done things in a spirit of Love. As memory scans the past, above and beyond all the transitory pleasures of life, there leap forward those supreme hours when you have been enabled to do unnoticed kindnesses to those round about you, things too trifling to speak about, but which you feel have entered into your eternal life. I have seen almost all the beautiful things God has made; I have enjoyed almost every pleasure that He has planned for man; and yet as I look back I see standing out above all the life that has gone four or five short experiences when the Love of God reflected itself in some poor imitation, some small act of love of mine, and these seem to be the things which alone of all one's life abide. Everything else in all our lives is transitory. Every other good is visionary. But the acts of Love which no man knows about, or can ever know about—they never fail.

In the Book of Matthew, where the Judgment Day is depicted for us in the imagery of One seated upon a throne and dividing the sheep from the goats, the test of a man then is not, "How have I believed?" but "How have I loved?" The test of religion, the final test of religion, is not religiousness, but Love. I say the final test of religion at that great Day is not religiousness, but Love; not what I have done, not what I have believed, not what I have achieved, but how I have discharged the common charities of life. Sins of commission in that awful indictment are not even referred to. By what we have not done, *by sins of omission*, we are judged. It could not be otherwise. For the withholding of Love is the negation of the Spirit of Christ, the proof that we never knew Him, that for us He lived in vain. It means that He suggested nothing in all our thoughts, that He inspired nothing in all our lives, that we were not once near enough to Him to be seized with the spell of His compassion for the world. It means that—

"I lived for myself, I thought for myself,
   For myself, and none beside—
   Just as if Jesus had never lived,
   As if He had never died."

It is the Son of *Man* before whom the nations of the world shall be gathered. It is in the presence of *Humanity* that we shall be charged. And the spectacle itself, the mere sight of it, will silently judge each one. Those will be there whom we have met and helped; or there, the unpitied multitude whom we neglected or despised. No other Witness need be summoned. No other charge than lovelessness shall be preferred. Be not deceived. The words which all of us shall one Day hear sound not of theology but of life, not of churches and saints but of the hungry and the poor, not of creeds and doctrines but of shelter and clothing, not of Bibles and prayerbooks but of cups of cold water in the name of Christ. Thank God the Christianity of to-day is coming nearer the world's need. Live to help that on. Thank God men know better, by a hairsbreadth, what religion is, what God is, who Christ is, where Christ is. Who is Christ? He who fed the hungry, clothed the naked, visited the sick. And where is Christ? Where?—whoso shall receive a little child in My name receiveth Me. And who are Christ's? Everyone that loveth is born of God.

Afterword

THE ANALYSIS OF LOVE

In any survey of the most influential devotional books in the English language, three would, without question, come near the top of the list—Augustine's *Confessions*, John Bunyan's *Pilgrim's Progress* and Thomas à Kempis' *Imitation of Christ*. Were a fourth nomination sought, there are those who would claim it could only be one of the spiritual classics of all time—Henry Drummond's *The Greatest Thing in the World*.

There is a solid basis for this claim. What other devotional book has, as Drummond's has, sold by the million? Records of its sales from its first appearance in 1890 do not exist—according to the main publishers of the book, but from two publishing houses (one was The Drummond Press in Drummond's home town of Stirling in Scotland) there came the assurance: "Over a million sold by this press alone." The other states that, even since 1950, 1,226,883 copies of *The Greatest Thing in the World* have been sold by them. To be added to that is the number of copies that have gone round the world through translations. So with figures that run into "millions" there is indeed validity in the claim made by John Birkbeck, then Director of The Drummond Press, in *A Mirror set at the Right Angle* that Drummond, in terms of "honest thinking" and "the joyful practice of religion", "merits equal veneration" with "great saints like Augustine, Bernard and Francis".

The Greatest Thing in the World is an exposition of St Paul's momentous chapter on Love in his first letter to the Corinthians, the famous Chapter 13. It was, on the first occasion that it was given, a spontaneous address on the Hymn of Love offered to an invited audience on a garden lawn in Kent in a human situation that became an historic one.

Dwight L. Moody, the great American preacher for ever linked with Ira D. Sankey in their evangelistic team, was due to address that audience. Tired after eight months' "solid preaching", Moody told his audience he had "given all he had to give" and so he wanted them to hear "a substitute recently returned from Africa, Henry Drummond". Drummond took out his pocket Bible, read I Corinthians 13 and then quietly and confidently proceeded to give the analysis of Love that the world has come to know as *The Greatest Thing in the World*. He gave the address again—by request—when he received the degree of Doctor of Law at Amherst, Connecticut, as his response to that honour. Then, because much of his work had been "pirated" in the U.S.A. and "baptised by titles the author never conceived", he himself prepared the book for publication in all its aspects—layout, cover design, proof-reading, etc., to ensure that its effect on eye and mind were equally pleasing. From that time on, *The Greatest Thing in the World* has blessed millions and been the agent of manifold miracles of grace.

The medium of such a message can only be a remarkable man of the Spirit. That he was indeed remarkable is borne out by the estimates made of him by those who knew him. There was the testimony of a friend of many years: "The most perfect Christian I have ever seen or expect to see this side of the grave." There is the testimony of Sir George Adam Smith: "He was one of the purest, most unselfish, most reverent souls you ever knew." There is the tribute of Sir Archibald Geikie, then Director General of the Geological Survey of the United Kingdom: "I have never met with a

53

man in whom transparent integrity, high moral purpose, sweetness of disposition and exuberant helpfulness were more happily combined with wide culture, poetic imagination and scientific sympathies than they were in Henry Drummond." There is the simple statement from Sir James Young Simpson: "There is no known equivalent of such lustrous life."

These are sincere statements by those who knew him. Is their objectivity distorted by nearness, biased by admiration? Has time brought modification of such glowing estimates to the ministry of one man? It seems not, for John Birkbeck, writing eighty years later as an authority on his life and work, can say: "It is incontestible that in an age which wanted to see religion lived out, they saw it in the transparent character of this valiant Christian reflecting the sunshine of His faith. Those who write about him are at one in the conviction that the greatest thing about the man was the man himself. Men felt instinctively that what he said was true to the man who uttered it and that he was telling them of things through which he had lived and which were real to themselves."

"Religion lived out." It was this that so moved

Moody himself, for he saw *The Greatest Thing in the World* as in some way Drummond incarnate, for he wrote: "Some men take an occasional journey into the thirteenth chapter of I Corinthians, but Henry Drummond was a man who lived there constantly, appropriating its blessings and exemplifying its teachings. As you read what he terms the analysis of love, you found that all its ingredients were interwoven into his daily life, making him one of the most lovable men I have ever known." This was a man, certainly rare and probably unique.

Who was this remarkable Henry Drummond?

Drummond was born in Stirling in 1851. The family background provided an environment in which his own interests and gifts could root and grow. The family business was close to the nature he came to love and study deeply—A. S. Drummond & Sons, the family firm of which both his father and grandfather were the chief officials, were seedsmen—while an uncle on his mother's side was James Blackwood, a minerologist greatly concerned with scientific matters. The presence and influence of "natural law" was early with him. His father, Henry Drummond senior, as well as being a successful business man, came, especially in his later life, prominently into religious work. He taught in Sunday school, was President of the Young Men's Christian Association, served as an elder in the North Church, Stirling, and founded a Sunday school at near-by Cambusbarron. His uncle Peter—through whom, under the Holy Spirit, Drummond was converted—created the well-known evangelical publishing agency, the Stirling Tract Enterprise.

So natural law and the spiritual world were essential elements in the early life of one who was to be remembered for his pioneer study of the relationship of science and religion—the famous *Natural Law in the Spiritual World*.

It was with a love for geology and science that he left school. It was also with a sense of call to God's service that he could not define. A normal boy— normal in the sense that he enjoyed and participated in all the activities of school and university, including sport—there was nevertheless something about Drummond that clearly separated him from others. He was different. He was involved in every part of life and had a great love for people, but there was that distance about him that, in the case of His Lord and Master, made Mary see much, say little, but "ponder it all in her heart". Ralph Connor, in an article in *British Weekly* in 1903, seems to be referring to just that when he writes: "He had a mysterious aloofness that made one feel he had a world of his own into which none could quite enter." Perhaps this is the essential mark of those elected to special service. Drummond was no saint, in the plastic or stained-glass sense—as Sir George Adam Smith assures us. In other words, he was not some unworldly being, untouched (for he felt deeply his unworthiness and sinfulness) by the world. He was certainly in the world, but he was never of it, the disciple's proper position.

It was this something about his natural Christianity (Smith says that his most conspicuous service to his generation was his demonstration of Christianity as perfectly natural) that marked Drummond out for special service to Christ's Kingdom, for, at the age of twenty-two he was, as J. Y. Simpson says, "swept into the greatest evangelistic movement of the century". Moody and Sankey came to Scotland with the Great Mission of 1873-75. Totally different from these American evangelists, Drummond nevertheless felt the sincerity of Moody and the importance of his new methods, particularly in terms of ministry to the individual. The consequences for Drummond were extraordinary. He found himself addressing thousands at a time, exercising an outstanding ministry to young men, writing major discourses (for example those published after his death as *The Ideal Life*), and exercising an outstanding personal ministry to an endless number of people from every walk of life. For a young student of twenty-two, the personal dangers were enormous, but, as Dr James Stalker, who shared so much of his work, wrote: "Henry retained the humility of self-forgetfulness throughout life." It was a supreme test—and perhaps a mark of his difference that he passed that crucial personal test.

Henry Drummond never became an ordained minister and indeed seemed to feel it essential that he should not be ordained. He was finally licensed to preach though he had resisted that too because of his uncertainty over a calling. His work as a student missionary in Possilpark, a suburb of Glasgow, made licensing desirable and he agreed to it. His ministry there—he was still in his twenties —was so outstanding that in 1882 the General

Assembly of the then Free Church raised the charge to full status and Drummond resigned his missionary post to enable an ordained minister to be appointed.

Perhaps it was the flexibility non-ordination gave—for ordination and full charge of a church impose limits—that allowed him to pursue his scientific studies and research in the Rocky Mountains in 1879, in Central Africa in 1883–84, and in the New Hebrides in 1891. There he lost himself in geological exploration and the study of natural law and found too, especially in his African experience, the reality of suffering.

It is not my purpose to write here the biography of this notable Christian. The major biography by Sir George Adam Smith (*The Life of Henry Drummond*) provides that and others (such as J. Y. Simpson's *Henry Drummond* in the Famous Scots Series) paint graphically his extraordinary ministry —unordained as he remained. As lecturer and professor of Natural Science in Glasgow's Free Church College, as preacher, evangelist, spiritual director, writer, Boys' Brigade official (a movement dear to his heart), his influence was vast. And yet in all, he was but forty-three when he died in 1897.

Where lies the secret of Henry Drummond?

There is a remarkable passage that opens the door to an understanding of Drummond's fundamental convictions. It comes from a period in which Drummond was under suspicion in evangelical circles, not least the evangelical circles from which he sprang. The famous heresy hunt that pursued Professor Robertson Smith, because of his belief that the Holy Spirit was at work as much in the critical as in the experimental use of the Bible, and that the Church was being led nearer to truth through the work of criticism, impinged on Drummond. *The Ascent of Man*, in particular, was judged by many to be dangerously unorthodox. Moody was quick to spring to his defence ("I have read every line of his books, and have never read a word with which I have disagreed") while Sankey wrote to Drummond in Glasgow, enclosing a newspaper cutting of an address the latter had given. Sankey was anxious that Drummond should re-affirm this statement. That crucial and profound passage reads:

"The power to set the heart right, to renew the springs of affection, comes from Christ. The sense of the infinite worth of the single soul, and the recoverableness of man at his worst, come from Christ's Cross; the hope of immortality springs from Christ's grace ... Personal conviction means for life a personal religion, a personal trust in God, a personal dedication to His cause. These, brought about how you will, are supreme things to aim at, supreme losses if they are missed."

Drummond replied: "These are my words, and there has never been an hour when the thoughts which they represent were not among my deepest convictions."

The Greatest Thing in the World comes out of a man with that depth of conviction. *Love* is the *summum bonum*, love above all things. He contrasts it ("The Contrast") with other things greatly valued, but obviously inferior—eloquence, prophecy, sacrifice and martyrdom. Without Love, there is no profit for anyone. He offers "The Analysis"—"an amazing analysis of what this supreme thing is"—and sets out "The Spectrum of Love" with its nine ingredients—Patience, Kindness, Generosity, Humility, Courtesy, Unselfishness, Good Temper, Guilelessness and Sin-

THE ANALYSIS OF LOVE

cerity. He closes with "The Defence". "Love is the supreme possession: *it lasts*."

Henry Drummond will be remembered for his immense efforts in *Natural Law in the Spiritual World* and *The Ascent of Man* to show that "science without religion was blind and did not know *where* to go, and that religion without science was lame and did not know *how* to go." Birkbeck, who thus summed up Drummond's works, adds: "He sought to make plain the dependence of each on the other." But the deeper memories still will be of the natural Christian who took his stand on "the old factors—the living Spirit of God, the living Word of God, the old Gospel". "The business of the preacher is not to prove things," said Drummond, "but to make people see them."

Henry Drummond has done just that in *The Greatest Thing in the World* and will continue to do it through the continuing witness of this classic book. But perhaps his contemporaries would exhort all who read this great work to see that Love, "the greatest thing in the world", was somehow impressively real in this rare Christian man.

Denis Duncan